# Stirrir

GW01417924

## Abby Grubb

‹

**BookLeaf Publishing**

Presentation by *BookLeaf Publishing*

Web: www.bookleafpub.com

E-mail: info@bookleafpub.com


ISBN: 9789357442350

First edition 2023

*For my parents who have inspired me to reach for the stars.*


*For my older sister who taught me to embrace my uniqueness.*


*For my older brother who is the quiet voice of reason.*


*For my brother in-law who has become a second brother.*


*For my nephews who remind me the simple things matter most in life.*

# ACKNOWLEDGEMENT

To my high school English teacher Mr Finnigan who encouraged me to pursue my dreams in the writing field.

To my college lecturer Rona who gave me a new perspective to my writing.

To my university lecturer Manos who helped develop my poetry writing skills.

# PREFACE

I am delighted to share my poems for the first time with a public audience. Writing poems for me is a cathartic method of writing and usually helps me to process my emotions. This collection of poems is largely inspired by works of literature, films and various other creative works which I have encountered in my past or present.

# Airs and Graces

I am the youngest of seven daughters,
We have no fortune or land to our name,
The family home is in backwaters,
Nothing except lady luck is to blame.

My life revolves around balls and dances,
Constantly observed and on a tight leash,
Knowing looks pass and subtle advances,
I have no choice but to obey, capeesh?

Dignity and pride dictate every move,
Love means nothing to me, it's do or die,
I am a woman with something to prove,
I struggle in vain daring to just try.

I dance and I smile, but it's all a mask,
Dreaming of change would be too much to ask.

# Seven Sins

There are seven deadly sins,
Pride comes first,
Greed is fit to burst,
Lust playfully grins,
Envy rears its ugly head,
Gluttony staggers into the room,
Wrath arrives with its doom,
Sloth wants to go to bed.

Best to put others before you,
Be charitable and giving,
Stay pure and chaste,
Be grateful for the few,
Abstain while living,
Be patient and diligent without haste.

# St Emmeline of Caledonia

Emmeline was young, pious and devout,
She had a pretty face and golden hair,
Her family gathered all about,
As her beauty filled the air.

Without a single care,
She left the farm,
With a certain flair,
Certain she'd come to no harm.

The devil himself grabbed her arm,
She screamed, but no one could hear,
He worked his wicked charm,
She shed not a single tear.

She died on a sunny day,
Declared a Saint, go ahead and pray.

# Pet Psychic

Go beyond what you cannot see,
I'll take you by the hand,
You can trust me,

This is far from planned,
It's real if you believe so,
The process is hardly grand.

I'm a true and certified pro,
I can speak with your pet with my mind,
Tell me what you wish to know.

There's no pet I can't find,
Lost, deceased, misbehaving or ill,
Everything is intertwined.

# The Modern God

God means something different to every woman
and man,
Most say that he's blonde haired with ocean blue
eyes,
Some say he's all seeing and all knowing,
He can perform miracles, of course he can,
Resides in the heavens up in the skies,
His abilities just keep on flowing.

I think that God isn't even a male,
That's part of his mysterious guise,
Her ego keeps growing and growing,
That's the reason why she cannot fail.

Her eyes are glowing.

# Vindictive Higher Power

Everything is easier for the male race,
They are rewarded for simply being,
Their lives are far more freeing,
Even when they don't have a pretty face,
They always just have a place,
God Almighty isn't seeing,
He must surely be fleeing,
Vanished without a trace.

Life as a woman is far from being easy,
Expectations are impossibly high,
God laughs at our pain,
His ignorance makes me queasy,
He refuses to even cry,
Makes you wonder if he has a brain.

# Dance with the Devil

It's easy to fall from grace,
All it takes is a firm push,
A slap or spit in your face,
Men telling you to shush,
Keep your head down,
Hide that little frown.

I have lost my love of God,
Clearly, he's also flawed,
A devil whispered in my ear,
He said, "Come dance, dear",
I grinned and grabbed his hand,
"Please take me away from this land",
He promised me the world and more,
His promise touched me to the core.

# Opposite Day

Do run in the hall,
Don't do your chores,
Always start wars,
Take your eye off the ball.

Allow extended screen time,
Stay inside more,
Open the door,
Drop the slime.

Eat plenty of junk food,
Check that phone,
Loudly groan,
Be rude.

Please do tell a big lie,
Don't be willing to learn,
Waste what you earn,
Keep asking why.

# The Female Visionary

Mystics claim they see the future,
They call themselves visionaries,
As in they are blessed with divine visions from
God,
Joan of Arc is one of the most famous.

She herself was "A Maid",
Since the age of 13,
She has seen divine things,
Saints sent from God.

Some call her a heretic,
Others say she's a saint,
Not everyone is sure,
Now we say she's a female visionary.

She surpassed her class and gender,
Fought for her nation,
Empowered the female gender,
All while being a mere youth.

A female visionary for sure,
A true warrior of Christ,
A patriotic martyr,
Unworthy of the men who killed her.

# Sounds that Shape us

Sounds play a role in our life,
From the quiet to the loud,
Whispers to a noisy crowd,
Ones that cut like a knife.

Drip drop, raindrops fall,
A sound that soothes,
Swish, a sound that moves,
An early morning bird call.

Sounds that follow you wherever you go,
From natural to fake,
Since dawn to dusk,
Some up high and others down low,
When you sleep and when you wake,
Subtle sounds and one's that are brusque.

Sounds we all know,
Ones we can make,
Slowly starting to grow,
Sounds that can break,
Ones that even glow,
Out by the lake.

# Heretic

The English call me Joan of Arc,
My story has left a mark,
My visions have created a spark,
Like lightning in the dark,
My legacy is stark,
As infamous as Noah's ark,
Become a saint at last, hark,
My bite isn't as bad as my bark.

They tried to take my men's sark,
Claimed I only told lies,
Even said I spoke to the Devil,
My mission has become a snark,
Nobody heard my cries,
These judges aren't on my level.

Now I watch from on high as they revel,
Passive as they erect a new neville,
Scoff at man's so called evol.

# Misunderstood

An only child,
Manipulative father,
Upbringing was wild,
A passive mauther.

My name is Draco,
My family is whacko,
Father has all these opinions,
He follows Voldemort's minions.

I wish my life was like his,
Harry has it all,
His friend Hermione is a whiz,
Maybe that's why we brawl.

Misunderstood, that's what I am,
I am the boy who had no choice,
My cool persona is all a sham,
I should listen to my inner voice.

# Place in Time

Place means an area, position, or point,
This could be a certain location,
As useful and vital as a joint.

Place is important to our nation,
We often forget they are there,
They are a firm station.

Our place in time has a flair,
It's then, here and will,
Thinking of it is rare.

Everybody knows the drill,
Place is everywhere you go,
It never stands still.

Place has become a status quo,
It's there, even when it doesn't show.

# Right and Wrong

Right and wrong, a tricky thing,
Different to us all,
Large to some and to others small,
Some of us tightly cling,
What do we all bring?
It can cause a downfall,
Or maybe even a brawl,
I wonder what that thief can swing.

To an angel, a man can do no wrong,
Not even when he moves in for the kill,
Mankind is not without their faults,
To a demon, mankind is far from strong,
Of our crimes and sins, they have their fill,
Angel and demon are in a never-ending waltz.

# Sounds from the Deep

If you listen close to the ground,
There are all sorts of sounds to hear,
A whole new world can be found,
The number is sheer.

Sounds that many fear,
Scratching at your ears,
Some aren't clear,
Others produce tears.

Sounds that change over the years,
Evolving into ones we like,
Slowly grinding, shifting gears,
Suddenly rising, causing a spike.

Listen closely to the sounds from the deep,
Afterwards try and get a good night's sleep.

# Joseph, Mary and the Saviour

Joseph was a humble carpenter and didn't have
much money,
Mary was a young innocent, pious and beautiful
young virgin,
Something strange would soon happen to them,
something funny,
Inexplicable to man, animal, even to the smartest
surgeon.

Mary fell pregnant out of the blue,
Joseph saw an angel before him,
A remarkable baby was soon due,
The universe will sing a hymn.

The Saviour was soon born in a stable,
Three wise men gave him presents,
This is more than just a fable,
The world will remember these events.

A baby holds the fate of the world in his hands,
He has such incredible plans.

# Cautious Suffering

Justice must be served to the fair,
When do we draw the line?
Between what is good and bad,
Who deserves to be jailed there?

The line we draw is very fine,
It can sometimes drive us mad,
The evil deserves to rot in Hell.

It can make many people sad,
Both good and evil intertwine,
Perhaps, we shouldn't dwell,
We should appreciate what we once had.

# The Struggling Artist

A dark room, here he lies,
An artist and all his woes,
How he survives, nobody knows,
Look at the pained look in his eyes,
He can barely even rise,
Cannot even change his clothes,
Never mind churn out prose,
These lows ain't worth the highs.

The struggling artist lets out a sigh,
He rolls over and looks out the gap,
The sun is setting, he must move,
He glares at the reddening sky,
If only work would fall into his lap,
He needs to get out of this groove.

# Dream of the Manger

The witching hour tolls three,
I had a dream, strange and holy,
The manger where Christ lay spoke,
It consumed me wholly,
My sense of self broke,
It spoke with glee.

Creaking with age,
I rock to and fro,
Careful with the Lord,
I fear I'm not fit for this duty,
To bear his heavenly glow,
Upon this mortal stage,
To witness his eternal beauty,
I reluctantly take up the sword.

# Haves and Have Nots

In life there are two kinds of people,
The Haves who have it all,
The Have nots who have zero,
The two rarely ever cross.

The latter has seen loss,
Climbed the highest steeple,
They dream of a hero,
To catch them before they fall.

The former has no fear,
Holds their head up high,
Struts through life,
Without any care.

They can't see the doom that's nigh,
Their destruction is very near,
As their sins are so rife,
That will ruffle their perfect hair.

# Miracles

Christ wandered the land,
Performing amazing deeds,
Fulfilling everyone's needs,
Taking the lost by the hand,
Making a righteous stand,
Planting all kinds of seeds,
Uprooting any unwanted weeds,
His father had this all planned.

He made the blind see,
Cured the terminally ill,
Filled the poor with glee,
All by using his will,
His miracles were never wee,
This was never for the thrill.

His hands wouldn't kill,
His deeds were a show,
To prove what he did know.

Milton Keynes UK
Ingram Content Group UK Ltd.
UKHW020634130923
428592UK00015B/599

9 789357 442350